BYGONES OF BEXHILL

by

SHIRLEY READ

MEADOWBRIGHT BOOKS
East Sussex

Published by:
MEADOWBRIGHT BOOKS
14 Mitten Road
Bexhill-on-Sea
East Sussex
TN40 1QL

ISBN 0-9520191-0-8
Drawings and maps by the author

British Library Cataloguing-in-Publication Data
A catalogue record for this book is available from the British Library

Origination by   Shirley and Alan Read

Printed by :   **WNA Printers**
                    3a Terminus Road
                    Bexhill-on-Sea
                    East Sussex TN39 3LP

        Tel: 0424-222538

BYGONES OF BEXHILL

List of Contents

My thanks to the many Bexhillians who, through their conversations and writings, have helped in the preparation of this Introduction to the History of the Town.

Dedicated to Lawrence

PRE-HISTORY

One of Bexhill's earliest residents - over sixty-five million years ago - is likely to have been the iguanodon. A member of the dinosaur family (also known as Terrible Lizards), he was so called because his fossilised teeth (first discovered in Sussex in 1822) were very like those of the iguana, a South American lizard.

The iguanodon was between twenty-five to thirty feet from head to tail and several tons in weight. Despite a fearsome appearance, he was a peaceable fellow feeding off the lush vegetation in Bexhill's then sub-tropical climate. Footprints of the iguanodon can be seen embedded in the soft sand near Galley Hill when the tide is low. With three toes, they are two feet wide and one and a half long. Casts of them are in Bexhill Museum.

Other early residents of whom there is evidence include Neolithic Man, from about 6000 years ago. Traces of his tools and weapons have been found locally on Bexhill Down and at Ashburnham, Ninfield and Lunsford Cross. The Bronze Age people were also here about 2000BC. Remains of a small open boat, possibly a fishing vessel, were discovered in Egerton Park when the lake was first dug in 1888. An oak coracle, some nine feet long, was unearthed from the clay near South Cliff at Cooden, and during the 1890s, various tools and arrowheads were found at Norman's Bay.

ROMAN AND SAXON INFLUENCES

The Roman's great port of Anderida, along the coast at Pevensey, was the main garrison post for the whole of Sussex and covered some nine acres. The Pevensey Levels formed an inland estuary during Roman times. This separated the hilly region between Cooden and Fairlight (known as the Hastings Peninsula) from the rest of the county. There were ironworks to the north, at places such as Ashburnham and Beauport Park, but, on the whole, it was a very thinly populated area.

The Romans left during the 5th century AD and by then the whole south-east coast was regularly invaded by bands of Saxons. Aella and his followers, from the German Baltic Coast, landed in the west, at Selsey, and marched eastwards. They reached Pevensey, but got no further. This was because another tribe, one of Jutish origin, led by Haesten, having made their way westwards from Kent, were settled here.

Apart from the small settlement by its natural harbour - the Romans had called it *Portus Novus*- it was a hard and inhospitable region. The thick, sandy forests covered the hilly terrain and reached right to the sea's edge, with rivers and marshlands to both east and west. At first Haesten and his followers relied mainly on the sea for their food. But it was not long before they had made a home for themselves and their powerful influences were reaching out beyond the Hastings Peninsula - across to Hastingleigh over the Kent border in the east, and along the forest ridges to Hastingford (near today's Hadlow Down) in the west.

For two hundred years, the Haestingas led an independent life, probably with their own dynasty. The Anglo-Saxon Chronicle talks more than once of "the men of Sussex, Kent and Hastings". Even after they were officially conquered by Offa, King of Mercia in 771, the Haestingas managed to keep at least some of their independence. As late as 1149, their tribal name was still being recorded.

By the 10th century, Hastings was a town of traders and craftsmen, boasting its own mint. The only places in the south-east with larger mints were London, Canterbury, Dover and Lewes. It had a fishing fleet, a good harbour and a number of ships (maybe as many as twenty), which were offered for sea service to the Crown. This brought the town special privileges and was the forerunner of the Cinque Ports Confederation. The Confederation played a vital part in defending the country against invasion, and, until the 15th century, its ships were the only navy England had.

The five original headports were Hastings, Romney, Hythe, Dover and Sandwich, with Rye and Winchelsea being added later as "Antient Towns". Each headport had its corporate members or "limbs". Those of Hastings were Pevensey and Seaford. Hastings' sphere of influence was equivalent to a third of today's County of East Sussex, and most certainly included the small hilltop village of Bexhill just along the coast.

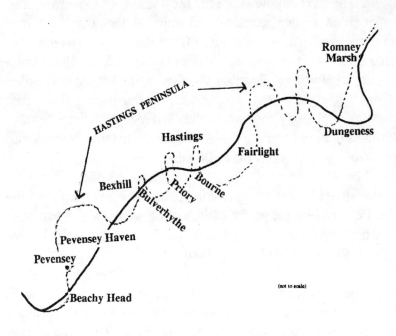

(Dotted line represents suggested early coastline)

THE NORMANS

During all the comings and goings across the Channel, Hastings developed strong ties with Normandy. Emma, daughter of the Duke of Normandy, was married to Ethelred II - known as the Unready - and later to Canute the Dane. Under Emma's influence, Canute endowed the Manors of Brede and Rameslie to the Abbey of Fecampe in Normandy. These manors covered much of the Hastings coastline across to Winchelsea.

Such connections are likely to have influenced William the Conquerer in his choice of invasion area. He set sail from St. Valery on the French coast on Thursday 27th September 1066. His army was carried in almost seven hundred flat-bottomed boats, his own vessel being called *The Mora*. The next day he landed somewhere near Pevensey. The precise spot is not known because the shoreline, although altered from Roman times, was still very different from the one we know today. The wide estuary of the Pevensey Haven lay between William and a direct route to Hastings. Possibly the fleet re-embarked and sailed across or maybe they went on foot along the high ground past Herstmonceux. Nobody knows how they arrived, but what is certain, the Normans did not bypass Bexhill, which by this time was a small village covering sixty hides or 1,200 acres.

It took the villagers more than twenty years to recover from all the damage. Fortunately, the parish church of St. Peter (which had been endowed by King Offa in 772 and, until the Reformation, was known as St. Peter and St. Paul) had survived.

A small tower was added by Robert, Count of Eu. He was a cousin of William, appointed by him as Lord of the Rape of Hastings (Sussex was divided into six such rapes, or divisions). Bexhill was towards the western edge of the Hastings Rape.

One theory says the name *Bexhill* comes from a Saxon word for "windy", but another tells us it derives from the Old English, *Byxeleah,* meaning "boxtree wood or clearing". The evergreen box *(Buxus semperivens)* grew abundantly across southern England, especially on hillsides. Other place names such as Bexley in Kent and Box Hill in Surrey also record this fact. The 8th century version of Bexhill is *Bexlea* or *Bixlea*, but, later, the second element, "leah", was confused with "hill". By 1086, the name is written as *Bexelei*; in 1278, it is *Bixel*, and in 1496, *Byxhell*. *Bexhill* became the accepted form once spelling was standardised. The *-on-Sea* was added only a hundred years ago when the modern resort was developed.

In Norman times, Bexhill had not turned its face to the sea. The village clustered round St. Peter's Church on its hill 150ft above sea level, and the sea itself was a long way off. Much of the intervening land was marshy and the higher ground of Galley Hill and South Cliff and, between them, The Horn (the site now of the De La Warr Pavilion) extended a lot further seawards. Several streams flowed down from Battle and Sidley, entering the sea at various points between Bulverhythe and Norman's Bay. The area, offering rough grazing for cattle, was full of wildfowl. In bad weather, heavy seas swept right up to where St. Barnabas Church in Sea Road and the Sackville Arch now stand.

So, instead of bothering about such a desolate area, the Bexhillians of those days looked towards the ridge of higher ground leading from Bulverhythe and Hastings. There was Sidley to the north, a quite separate hamlet, possibly older than Bexhill itself. Westwards lay Bexhill Down and beyond that, Pevensey Haven, with the South Downs as a backdrop in the far distance.

THE MANORS OF THE BEXHILL HUNDRED

The Bexhill Hundred was one of thirteen in the Rape of Hastings. Each hundred, according to the Domesday Book compiled in 1086 by William the Conqueror, consisted of groups of manors, or pieces of land, varying in size, and held by tenants under a single landlord.

The Manor of Bexhill was some twenty hides, with land for about twenty-six ploughs. Its value before the Conquest was £20, afterwards it was nil, and by 1086, it had risen again to £18.10s (£18.50p.). Three of the hides were kept by the Count of Eu for his own use, and he leased ten others to Osbern, a farmer of some note. The remaining seven hides were divided between six other tenants - in amounts varying between a half and two-and-a-half hides - and the two clerics of St. Peter's Church, who were Geoffrey and Robert. There were no more than eighty people, consisting mostly of villagers and cottagers, in Bexhill at this time.

In 1148, Count Robert's grandson, John, gave the Manor of Bexhill back to the Church. He kept other lands, which later became the Manors of Buckholt and Cooding, and their ownership was handed down with the Lordship of the Rape.

Buckholt passed to the Fiennes family of Herstmonceux, later becoming part of the Normanhurst estates. These belonged to the Brassey family, who, in turn, were linked by marriage to the Sackvilles. The Brassey connections with both Hastings and Bexhill are well-established.

Thomas Brassey made the family fortune by constructing railways all over the world, and his eldest son became the 1st Baron (then Earl) Brassey. He lived at Beauport Park and was MP for Hastings during the 1870s and 80s. Later, he was Bexhill's first honorary freeman and elected Mayor.

Cooden belonged to the Coding family. A fine moated house was built in the 13th century, but now only the moat remains and a very sorry sight it is. For the curious, it can be found along a footpath leading off Maple Walk. The Coding family died out in the early 1500s and ownership of the Manor later passed to the Sackvilles, thus linking it with the Manor of Bexhill.

Cooden Beach golf course was laid out in 1912 on part of the old Cooden Manor. Before the Cooden Beach (now Resort) Hotel was opened in 1931, the site had been occupied by the largest barn in the district.

Battle Abbey received tithes from the Manors of Buckholt, to the north, and, to the west, Barnhorn. William de Northeye rented the park for hunting on payment of ``one fat deer and one fox net'' each year.

During the 15th century, Buckholt was held by William Batesford and then by his daughter, Joan, who left money in her will for the Batesford Chantry, a memorial to her parents, in St. Peter's Church. She was Lady Joan Brenchley who also held the Manor of Pebsham, to the east, and who was linked by marriage to the Manor of Cooden, to the west.

Northeye's original chapel, just north of the Barnhorn Road, was probably Bexhill's second church mentioned in the Domesday Book. It was on high ground, now known as Hill (previously Constable's) Farm, to the west of the old Prison.

The small port of Northeye, a Liberty of Hastings, was further south. It was ravaged by severe storms in the 13th century (which affected so much of the local coastline). Later, a new access to the Pevensey Sluice was cut for the Ashbourne River, which brought down the iron shipments from Ashburnham Forge. Stephen Waller, on behalf of the Pevensey Level Commissioners, did the work and it is still known as Waller's Haven. Pevensey Sluice, which took over from Northeye as a Liberty of Hastings, has been renamed Norman's Bay.

The Manor of Bexhill passed into Crown hands in 1561 and Elizabeth I then gave it to Thomas, son of Sir Richard Sackville of Buckhurst, who owned Knole House at Sevenoaks. He was also created Baron Buckhurst (the name came from the old family estate) and later raised to the earldom of Dorset.

Several generations later, the 7th Earl was created Duke of Dorset and appointed as Lord Warden of the Cinque Ports. But by 1843, the titles were extinct and the estates passed to the 3rd Duke's daughters.

The elder daughter, Mary, married the Earl of Amherst and when she died in 1864, all the lands went to her younger sister, Elizabeth, who married the 5th Earl De La Warr. It was through this marriage that the Manor of Bexhill and the estate of Buckhurst came into the De La Warr family, and so they remain to the present day.

THE DE LA WARRS

The De La Warr family came from the West Midlands. Roger La Warr was the 1st Baron in 1299. The title later passed to a nephew who was also the 3rd Baron West. It was this nephew's son who added the *De* to the La Warr title. The Wests also brought the Cantelupe name into the family. The mother of the 1st Baron West was the daughter of Sir John Cantelupe of Devonshire.

In the names of modern Bexhill, we find Cantelupe, along with others like Buckhurst, Dorset, Amherst, Devonshire as well as De La Warr itself, duly commemorated.

In the 16th century, the 9th Baron adopted a nephew as his heir, but the young man was too impatient for his inheritance and tried to poison his uncle. This resulted in his banishment, with the baronies of De La Warr and West falling into abeyance. After eighteen years' redeeming service in the French Wars, the once-erring nephew was created the 1st Baron De La Warr.

His grandson, the 3rd Baron, became Governor and Captain-General of the Colony of Virginia in 1610, and gave his name to the State of Delaware, one of the founder members of the USA. The 7th Baron was an army general who became Governor of New York and who in 1737 was made Viscount Cantelupe and Earl De La Warr.

Bexhill's link with the De La Warrs started in 1813 when the 5th Earl married Lady Elizabeth Sackville.

Martello Towers

SMUGGLING AND THE AMSTERDAM

By 1700, the Cinque Ports Confederation was having problems, with its harbours silting up and protective headlands being washed away. Smuggling, which had been going on for hundreds of years, now became an ever-tempting prospect. Wool was taken abroad, and brandy and lace shipped back. Later, all kinds of other goods, such as tea and tobacco, joined the list.

Few people lived near the edge of the sea, and the sands were far more extensive in those days. It was a simple matter for small boats to land on a moonless night and for the goods to be carried away on men's backs or in carts and coaches - the horses having their hooves muffled - along the beach at low tide.

A favourite landing spot was the site of the Queen's Hotel, Hastings and another was where Warrior Square, St. Leonards, is now. In Bexhill, Sea Lane (now Road) was used to bring contraband up to the Bell Inn.

Places were given nicknames to keep them secret. The Royal Victoria Hotel, St. Leonards, is on the site of a pool with overhanging rock, known as *Old Woman's Tap*, and near Galley Hill, there was a large rock called *Jinn's Stool*.

Dominating much of the local coastline was the notorious Hawkhurst Gang. Another was the Hastings Outlaws, or Transports. At Pevensey, gangs from Little (once known as Slyder's) Common used inns like The Star at Norman's Bay as their headquarters. From here, they carried goods inland to villages on the fringe of the Levels.

Bulverhythe was another Liberty of Hastings - its name means "Port of the People" - and one of the smugglers' favourite landing places. In January, 1748, it saw excitement of a most unusual kind when, during a very heavy storm, the Dutch East Indiaman, *The Amsterdam*, got into difficulties out in Pevensey Bay.

It was her maiden voyage and she was supposed to be on her way to Capetown. But instead, with her rudder torn off and upwards of fifty of her crew dead or dying from a fever, she ran aground off Bulverhythe. William Thorpe, Mayor of Hastings, wary of smugglers, put a guard on the ship and waited for soldiers to come from along the Sussex coast and from London. As soon as the tide was right, he helped Willem Klump, *The Amsterdam*'s Captain, take off the ship's silver, which was then stored in Hastings Customs House. Some of the sick were also removed, but many of the crew, having broken into the liquor store, were too drunk to worry about being trapped inside the stricken ship and stayed on board.

The storms raged all night and by morning *The Amsterdam* had sunk deeper into the sand. Lots of people from Hastings and Bexhill were on the beach, battling against the driving wind and rain, to see what was going on. Local wreckers and smugglers swarmed round the ship in several feet of water, armed with long poles with hooks on the end. They grabbed whatever they could - tea, beef, bacon, butter, velvet, gold and silver.

A gang from Hooe made off with some bales of cloth, but William Thorpe spotted their exploits and sent them home empty-handed. He must have been relieved when the soldiers arrived later that day to take over guardianship of the wreck.

The Amsterdam soon lay deeper in the sand and access was possible only at the lowest tide. Over the years, the locals tried time and again to dig down, but so waterlogged was the sand that nobody could manage more than a few feet.

The first serious salvage attempt took place sixty years later. In 1810, when the King's German Legion was stationed in Bexhill, Colonel Halkett gave permission for two hundred of his men to see what they could do. There was a theory that this number working together would

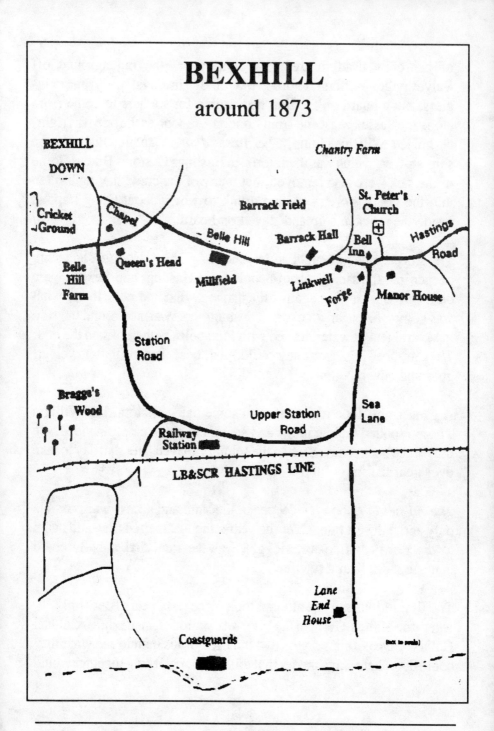

BEXHILL
around 1873

BEXHILL DOWN

Chantry Farm

Cricket Ground

Chapel

Barrack Field

St. Peter's Church

Belle Hill

Barrack Hall

Bell Inn

Hastings Road

Belle Hill Farm

Queen's Head

Millfield

Linkwell

Forge

Manor House

Station Road

Bragge's Wood

Upper Station Road

Sea Lane

Railway Station

LB&SCR HASTINGS LINE

Lane End House

(not to scale)

Coastguards

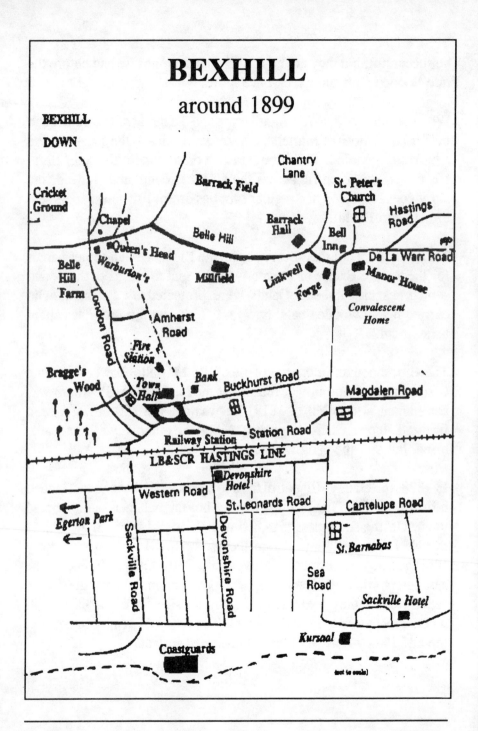

BEXHILL
around 1899

be successful, but they got no further than anyone else had before the tide flooded over the wreck once more.

With the Napoleonic Wars in full spate and the threat of invasion much increased, a series of Martello Towers was built and the coast became a lot better guarded. This brought extra problems for the smugglers, but the two-way traffic across the Channel continued. Indeed, the story goes Napoleon had regular supplies of English newspapers sent direct from Bexhill!

The smugglers did their best to bribe the Blockademen (other names for them were Excise or Preventivemen) sent to intercept them, and sometimes killed them. Gangs were protected by Batsmen, who carried heavy wooden bats, two yards long, with no scruples about using them.

The Blockademan in charge of Bexhill's Martello Tower (later the Coastguards' Station, near the site of the De La Warr Pavilion) was entertained at the Bell in 1819. He was offered £50 down, with a further £50 promised if he agreed to look the other way. A handsome bribe, but still the gang was betrayed.

In 1828, the Galley Hill patrol tried to stop a gang that had just landed near the Bo-Peep Inn at Bulverhythe, but the batsmen outnumbered them. Off the smugglers marched with their loot from Glyne Gap to the New Inn at Sidley. There they were met by a party of forty Blockademen, all armed, but even this made little difference. The smugglers killed the leader of the Blockademen, forcing the rest to retreat. Then they took refuge in Cramp's Farm off Holliers Hill where most were eventually caught. Ten received death sentences at the Old Bailey, but were later transported instead.

Pevensey witnessed the worst local battle in November 1833. The batsmen had guns as well as bats and cudgels this time. There was a running battle across the Marshes that lasted over two hours, with three of the gang killed and five taken prisoner. The rest escaped in the fog towards Wartling and Boreham Street. None of the Blockademen was injured and later they were each awarded £20 for their efforts.

KING'S GERMAN LEGION

A small military camp had been set up at Bexhill when soldiers were needed to help build the Martello Towers. The village population was around 2,000 and there was about a hundred houses. Imagine the impact the arrival, in 1804, of five or six thousand Hanoverian troops had on the place. There were four battalions of them - Bexhill had been chosen as an infantry depot!

The origins of the King's German Legion lay in defeat. The Elector of Hanover also happened to be George III of England. And when his army was beaten by the French, he appointed the troops as a separate force within the British Army.

The Legion camp stretched for twenty-five acres between Belle Hill, Chantry Lane and what is now London Road, with the parade ground running east to west. It was built on the north side of the hill, so that any Frenchmen lurking out to sea would not spot it. Later, the camp reached onto Bexhill Down, with outposts at Little Common. Major-

General Sir Arthur Wellesley (later the Duke of Wellington) was in command of the main brigade at Hastings. He came across to Bexhill and stayed in Barrack Hall, which was the officers' mess.

It was little wonder the Bexhillians of the early 19th century looked on all these troops and their noisy foreign ways with grave Sussex suspicion. They must have felt utterly swamped by the invasion. But, from all accounts, the German love of music broke the ice. The Legion's band soon became very popular and the locals realised the soldiers were but ordinary men far away from their own homes. The tradespeople were soon helping them in every way and the soldiers became a colourful part of village life.

After Napoleon's defeat at Waterloo in 1815, the King's German Legion was sent back to Hanover, taking with it not a few Bexhill brides, and much of the huge camp was demolished. After they had gone, the village must have felt very empty.

St Peter's Church

THE CHURCH AND MANOR HOUSE
The extra attention it had been receiving from the military meant that Bexhill now started to be *noticed* socially.

A contemporary newspaper described it as "one of the most healthy and pleasant situations on the coast of Sussex". Diplock's Guide to

Hastings told its readers: "Bexhill, about six miles to the west, is a most delightful morning ride along the coast. ... There is a good and convenient inn with every accommodation calculated for the reception of strangers who, in summer, are frequently induced to visit this rural spot." Now that the seaside had been made so fashionable by royal patronage, the first holidaymakers were about to descend on Bexhill!

A mile or so west of Hastings, on the site of Gensing Farm, James Burton built St. Leonards in 1828. Between there and Bexhill, there were probably no more than half a dozen houses and the narrow lane was edged in wild flowers and brambles. The village of Bexhill nestled among trees overlooking the breezy slopes leading to the sea. It had 1600 residents, an inn (the Bell), a few lodging houses, a small theatre (the Assembly Room), and, of course, the Manor House and St. Peter's Church.

Another fine feature was the lovely old walnut tree spreading its branches over the brow of Upper Sea Road (then Sea Lane). When the road was altered, the tree was given a protective circle of wrought-iron fencing atop a low brick wall, but later, when further alterations were made, it was necessary to cut the tree down. The stump was finally removed in 1921.

When the Count of Eu added the tower to St. Peter's, he had granted the church to the Collegiate Church of St. Mary's within the grounds of Hastings Castle. In return, it had a prebend, or share of the revenue, an arrangement that lasted until the 12th century when St. Peter's reverted to the See of Chichester. Much rebuilding has taken place over the years. The oldest parts are the tower, parts of the nave and the north chapel. In 1878, there was great excitement when an 8th century reliquary lid was dug out of the floor. This is a carved stone slab, full of early Christian symbolism. It is now mounted in a case on the church tower and known as *The Bexhill Stone*.

Formerly a seat of the Bishops of Chichester, the Manor House was so badly in need of repair by the 1960s that it had to be pulled down. Built of stone and covered in cement or plaster, much of it dated from the first Elizabethan age. After 1561, it was owned by the Sackvilles who added the Dorset wing. It was often empty and used only as a shooting lodge, for occasional visits. The estate stretched down the hill to where Manor and Magdalen Roads are now situated and towards Galley Hill.

During the 19th century, the Brook family, wealthy farmers in the area, acted as bailiffs and were often called "Squire" by the locals. They were also master of the hounds, and when in 1834, Princess Victoria (soon to become Queen) was staying with her mother, the Duchess of Kent, in Hastings, she drove to Bexhill and enjoyed a ride with the hounds.

When Viscount Cantelupe married in 1892, he decided to make the Manor House his home. It was beautifully restored and enjoyed ten splendid years as the focal point of Bexhill's society life.

The next occupant had German relatives living in Cologne and was forced to leave the country when the 1st World War started. Afterwards, the estate was bought by Sir Leicester Harmsworth, brother of the newspaper baron, Lord Northcliffe. He died in 1937 and his widow lived there until her death in 1963. Bexhill Corporation then purchased it for £23,000 and its possible future use was hotly debated. In 1968, along with South Lodge which fronted the High Street, it was declared unfit and pulled down.

The walled garden of the Manor House is still there, making a peaceful and pleasant oasis for residents and visitors alike, and there are also some reminders of the house itself. The outbuildings have become the Manor Barn, a hall for receptions and entertainment, and the Costume

Museum, a treasure trove of social and domestic life over the centuries.

THE BELL INN AND OTHER LANDMARKS

Sea Lane (now Upper Sea Road) led down to the railway in 1846. Having raced to reach Hastings before the South Eastern & Chatham Railway (SECR) got there first through Kent, the London, Brighton & South Coast Railway (LBSCR) opened their single coastal track that June. It ran across open countryside straight from Polegate to Pevensey and along to Bexhill and St. Leonards.

Nobody in those early days of steam fancied having the noisy, dirty engines coming too near their houses, because, quite apart from anything else, they might easily go beserk! So the line crossed the flat open fields a quarter of a mile or so from the Bell Inn and St. Peter's. The first tiny station, complete with picket fence and path linking it to Sea Lane, was on the north side of the track. This area later became a goods yard and is now Sainsbury's car park.

The station was subsequently moved to the south side of the railway line, opposite the Devonshire Hotel. A subway linked the two parts of the town until, in 1902, a footbridge was erected. (This was replaced in 1991, but the new bridge does not look like lasting nearly as long as the original!) In the same year, the station platforms were extended and a new booking hall and entrance were built, opening onto Sea Road.

The Bell Inn is an old posting house and for many years acted as a centre of village life. In 1888, it was renovated and given a new exterior. The only west-east road - a narrow, twisting one - through Bexhill ran outside its door. Via Little Common, the traveller came in past the Queen's Head and the old Wesleyan Chapel (now a nursery school). Then it was up Belle (originally Belly) Hill, bearing left to meet the Chantry Lane/High Street junction. Having gone the length of the High Street, he would then bear left past the top of Sea Lane, with the Bell on the corner of Church Street, along past the Manor House and onto the Hastings Road. In those days this swept in an arc on the high ground before joining Bulverhythe and St. Leonards. No arrow-straight De La Warr Road in those early days, and certainly no King Offa Way!

The forge that for years had stood at the top of Sea Lane was demolished in the late 1940s and only pictures of it remain. But Pococks, the butchers, is still thriving. This family business opened around 1770 and moved to the present premises in 1801. Behind the shop is the old slaughterhouse. It is easy to picture it all when the King's German Legion was billeted here.

A 15th century Wealden house stands nearby in Church Street, part of which is now an excellent restaurant known as "Lychgates".

To celebrate Queen Victoria's Golden Jubilee in 1887, a handsome clock was erected at the corner of the High and Church Streets. It was put on a warehouse building belonging to Cave Austin, the grocery firm with branches in Hastings and St. Leonards as well as Bexhill. Unfortunately, nineteen years later, in June 1908, a nasty fire badly damaged the warehouse and the clock was destroyed. Later that same year, on King Edward VII's birthday, a replica was ceremoniously put in place and is still there today. The restored warehouse is now an antiques centre.

Jubilee Clock

The tradition of the Old Bexhill Fair lasted well into the 19th century. A charter was granted in the reign of Edward II - between 1307 and 1327 - for a market to be held in Bexhill every Monday and for a fair to take place four times every year.

The original premises of Warburtons at 8 Belle Hill were demolished in 1975 when King Offa Way was constructed. Ebenezer Warburton, a corn and agricultural merchant, came over from Uckfield and bought the old corn stores in 1887. Later, a coal and wagon yard was built, and the adjoining bakery was taken over. In 1910, the Station Road premises were opened. Most of the firm's supplies came by rail and were delivered to the goods yard (now a car park) right next door. They included seed corn from East Anglia, beet pulp from Suffolk and straw from West Sussex. The merchandise has changed to meet altering life styles over the years, but the firm remains an established favourite and is now run by the great-grandson of the founder.

When the East Sussex Police Constabulary was formed in 1840, it had twenty-three men. Bexhill was part of the Battle Division that consisted of a superintendent and four constables, who were stationed at Robertsbridge, Guestling, Boreham Street and Northiam. Later, Bexhill came under the larger Hastings Division, which included Peasmarsh, Brede, Winchelsea and Ore. Bexhill then boasted its own police house in Belle Hill. Later, a small police station was built in Barrack Road and had two cells with accommodation for one sergeant.

Bexhill's first post office was also in Belle Hill, in a cottage attached to "Genista", the home of the Wallis family. It came under Hastings postal district until the 1st World War and issued post to Little Common. Later, the post office moved to the High Street in premises owned by the Reeves family, where it was combined with a bakery and general stores.

"Linkwell" is an imposing Regency house in the High Street. In its grounds was one of the deepest wells in the town, descending to a depth of one-hundred and twenty feet. This and others in the area supplied Bexhill's drinking water for many years.

The nasty typhoid, epidemic which struck the town in 1880, was caused by farm waste contaminating the well water. Dr. Wallis of "Genista" did much to campaign for better sanitation. Primitive sewer pipes dumped their contents in the fields below the town. The main outfall pipe was at the bottom of Belle Hill, from whence a little stream meandered its foul-smelling way across what is now Egerton Park to the sea.

Warburtons, Belle Hill

LOCAL GOVERNMENT, HEALTH AND EDUCATION

Bexhill's Board of Guardians was appointed by the Battle Poor Law Union, but it was clear to many locals that their wellbeing was not properly cared for. So, in 1884, in the Bell Inn Assembly Room, the Local Board of Bexhill was elected - the forerunner of local government in the town. Its first chairman was Lieut. Col. Henry Lane who was also the first JP and who later became Chairman of the Urban Council. His memorial can be seen, appropriately, on the green opposite the Town Hall.

The Local Board's first Clerk was F.A. Langham, a well-known Hastings solicitor who later became its mayor. As there was no office accommodation in Bexhill, he came across from Hastings in a pony and trap, bringing all the necessary books and papers with him each time.

Bexhill first levied rates for the care of its poor in 1737, and in June 1755, the sum of £500 was raised to build "a workhouse on land taken by leave of His Grace the Duke of Dorset". This was on the eastern side of Bexhill Down and known for a long time afterwards as Workhouse Field. King Offa Schools now occupy the site.

The parish overseers carried out all the everyday duties, such as hiring doctors and finding those without work jobs on local farms, but all the appointments had to be confirmed by the Divisional Magistrates in Hastings. All the money had to be banked there, too. (There was no bank in Bexhill until 1885 when the Tunbridge Wells bankers, Beeching, Hodgkin & Beeching, expanded their Hastings branch.) The workhouse was closed in 1834 and the elderly, poor and destitute were despatched to Battle Workhouse, now Battle Hospital. During the typhoid epidemic, there were some isolation huts on Bexhill Down, but the town was without any hospital facilities of its own until the 20th century. Patients had to go to Hastings to the Old Infirmary, first opened in 1841. This was replaced by the East Sussex Infirmary in 1887, the site of which is now occupied by the White Rock Theatre.

The Buchanan Hospital, St. Leonards, first opened its doors in 1881, in the same year as the Metropolitan Convalescent Institution in Bexhill. This was the first of many convalescent homes in the town and, for one-hundred and eight years, it enjoyed a most imposing position on the southern slopes of the Old Town, overlooking the Channel. It was demolished in 1989 to make way for new housing.

Bexhill's first schoolmaster was Thomas Pye, also the rector of St. Peter's for twenty years, from 1589 to 1609. He used the Chantry Chapel as his "schole house". Apart from a John Dann who was schoolmaster in 1775, no other details of education in the town are known until we reach the 1850s.

St. Peter's School, as a separate building, opened in Holliers Hill in 1853. Nine years later a girls' department was formed and later still, infants were allowed to attend. The school was assisted by the National Society for the Education of the Poor, but parents were expected to contribute a few pence each week. In 1885, separate schools for boys and girls were opened in Barrack Road.

In 1854, Bexhill came under the Hastings & St. Leonards Gas Company, yet no attempt was ever made by them to supply gas here. So, in 1885, the newly-formed Local Board supplied oil lamps to light the streets, and two years later, formed Bexhill's own gas company. Gasworks were built in Ashdown Road, on the De La Warr estate, and, within a year, all the oil lamps had been changed to gas ones. A procession was held to celebrate this splendid improvement. Electricity came to the town in 1900.

TOWARDS THE RAILWAY AND BEYOND

"Millfield", a house on the south side of Belle Hill, used to be known as "The Firs" and was owned by Samuel Scrivens. He married into a wealthy local family called Moorman and became the second largest landowner in the town. During the 1880s, he sold off farmland between Belle Hill and the coastal rail track. This led to the development of Station (now London) Road and the residential roads, such as Amherst, Chepborne, Windsor, Victoria, Reginald and Leopold, surrounding it.

The area between Holliers Hill and Wrestwood Road (formerly Haddocks Hill), where Cramp's Farm (refuge of those smugglers) had been, was built up by a Hastings syndicate in the 1870s.

The first sale of land from the De La Warr Estate was in 1880. This led to residential development in Hastings Road. But London Road was the first shopping area outside the Old Town. This was the initial step towards developing the slopes from the Old Town to the railway line.

The Town Hall, designed by Henry Ward of Hastings, was opened in 1895. The Lord Mayor of London made a special trip to Bexhill for the ceremony, with his sheriffs and state coach, and there was a magnificent procession through the town in celebration of the occasion.

In 1882, the 7th Earl De La Warr obtained a licence to build a sea wall and promenade on the eastern side of Sea Road. He engaged a South London builder, John Webb, to do the work and, in part-payment, gave him a stretch of empty land on the western side of Sea Road.

The De La Warr Parade was where the Kursaal, a most popular entertainments pavilion, was built in 1896. On Whit-Monday, it was opened by the Duchess of Teck, mother of the future Queen Mary (consort of King George V). Earl De La Warr sold it in 1908 and during the 1st World War it was renamed The Pavilion because people did not like its German connotations. It was pulled down in 1936 and Bexhill Sailing Club now occupies the site. Between 1895 and 1913 huge ornamental gates could close the De La Warr Parade off to traffic. Here, too, the very first motor racing trials in the country took place in 1902.

It was John Webb who laid out part of Egerton Park and its surrounding estate, as well as most of Western Road. He also built the Devonshire Hotel and in 1886 became its first licencee. This was the very first building south of the railway line. It was sold in 1892, enlarged in the late 1920s and for a long time was a main venue for meetings, dances and other functions.

A new station was built facing the Devonshire Hotel. This area was known as Station Square, but when the station entrance moved to Sea Road, it was renamed Devonshire Square and so it remains today.

The Sackville Arch until the 1890s was a narrow opening through which cattle reached their grazing ground on the seaward side. Once it was widened and modernised, it became another access point for Bexhillians to reach the new shops and housing developments south of the railway.

INTO THE 20TH CENTURY

The way was now clear for the *New Town* of Bexhill-on-Sea to be born and grow into the 20th century. In the 1880s, the population was around 2,300, but by the 1901 Census, it had risen to more than 12,000.

This was a huge increase in twenty years and indicates the scale of the building and development which went on as Victoria's reign came to an end and Edward VII's began.

The town could now boast its own newspaper. But it seems likely that most residents would soon have shortened the unwieldy title - *The Bexhill-on-Sea Chronicle and Visitors' List, Battle, Pevensey, Sidley and Little Common Advertiser*! In 1896 *The Bexhill-on-Sea Observer and Visitors' Register* put in its appearance, the two papers merging in 1930.

On the seafront, the Sackville Hotel was joined in 1895 by the Marine Hotel (now rebuilt as Dalmore Court) and two years later, by the Metropole, the site of which (it was bombed in World War II and had to be demolished) is now a putting green. Wilton Court was converted into flats after seventy years as a hotel, but the green-domed Granville Hotel in Sea Road still thrives after almost ninety years, having recently undergone a major refurbishment. The Northern Hotel, owned for three generations by the Sims family, is an original terrace of six late Victorian houses in Sea Road and a prime example of the town's architecture during this expansion period.

In 1902, a brand new railway station was built at West Bexhill and linked the town to the Hastings-Charing Cross route, across the splendid Crowhurst Viaduct. This met what most people think was an untimely end in the late 1960s after the line was closed. An electrically-driven tramway service opened in 1906 between St.

Crowhurst Viaduct

Leonards and Bexhill, later being extended to Cooden. The fare was three pence - a princely one penny in today's money!

All such expansions and developments - and those of the 20th century rate a book of their own - are indeed a very far cry from that iguanodon in his pre-historic swamp!